Good Hunting
Love Yo.

D1530779

The
Hunting Year

The Hunting Year

Alison Guest
and
Tony Jackson

© Alison Guest and Tony Jackson 1978

First published in 1978 by Barrie and Jenkins Ltd.
24 Highbury Crescent, London N5 1RX

All rights reserved. No part of this publication may be reproduced in any form or by any means without the prior permission of Barrie and Jenkins Ltd.

ISBN 0 214 20478 2

Printed litho in Great Britain by W & J Mackay Ltd, Chatham, Kent

Foreword

The Hunting Year is a book that holds your attention, and it comes from the pen of a knowledgeable countryman. Tony Jackson neither skirts round the ethics of the subject of fox hunting nor overlooks the details that illuminate the sport. As Director of the Society that has attempted to hold for nearly fifty years the political shield in defence of country sports I feel very honoured to be invited to write this Foreword.

Trotsky is alleged to have said that hunting acts on the mind like a poultice on a sore. The soundness of this is confirmed in this book as the author traces the hunting man's year. His involvement with friends, with horse and hound, and with the wild life of the land becomes an abiding passion. Hunting makes people happy. I know no other sport that quite achieves this and the old Army adage that fox hunting was good training for leadership had something in it too.

Tony Jackson states the truth when he says that the goodwill of the farming community is the keystone to foxhunting. The goodwill of the shooting community comes a very close second. The control of the fox will always link the interests of these two sports and I can never recollect a time when the co-operation and understanding of both was more necessary.

I hope this book with its delightful illustrations will be read by everyone who has an interest in the countryside.

April, 1978

Robin Brockbank
Director BFSS

Introduction

Possibly no subject is more calculated to incur heated argument, to create ill-feeling, to foster the town versus country image, than foxhunting. Peaceable, apparently sane adults, are transformed into raging fanatics, careless of appearance and language; self-control flies out of the window and middle-aged spinsters of hitherto unblemished character assume the role of vicious termagants.

I have seen a schoolmaster, a man of presumed moderate habits and language, pouring forth a torrent of abuse which turned even a hardened first whipper-in's ears red, while his companion, a housewife of matronly proportions, wielded a banner denouncing foxhunters with all the fervour of a tub-thumping revivalist.

There are few foxhunters who, today, have not encountered, at some time or another, either in the field or at a country show or fair, the opposition, loosely labelled 'antis'. They are at once a pest and a hindrance but, fortunately, their antics can usually be contained; few will risk venturing on private land so they are compelled to give vent to their feelings by banner-waving demonstrations and abuse at meets or spraying hounds with chemicals. In practice, the latter appears to have not the slightest effect, probably proving more offensive to the field than to the hounds.

Even in the last century, when foxhunting was basking in a golden euphoria of general goodwill from press and public alike, 'do-gooders' were penning letters to editors, expressing their revulsion at 'this sadistic and outmoded practice'. Today, the correspondents are no less energetic, bombarding provincial and national press with their own particular brands of the truth as they see it.

It is only fair to point out many antis are totally sincere in their beliefs, misguided though they are; others give not a curse in hell for animals or their welfare — some have probably never seen a living fox in their lives — merely accepting with alacrity the chance to jump on a bandwagon with a built-in cause.

Society in Britain today is composed for the most part of town and city dwellers; we are no longer, nor have we been for 150 years, a rural nation. Not that this is in any way a reflection upon those who, by force of birth or circumstances, must earn their livelihood from commerce or industry. It does, however, guarantee generations who have lost their attachment to the countryside of their ancestors. The wheel has turned full circle, for it is no longer the countryman who is despised as a bumpkin, but the townee who is pitied by the fortunate country dweller.

The majority of the urban population can maintain only a tenuous rural connection via the press, television and occasional forays through, but not into, the countryside. The old ways and customs are treated as anachronisms, the sports of our fathers, evolved over the centuries, are now to be proscribed by those who, in their unseeing ignorance, can neither accept understanding nor toleration. Opinion on both sides solidifies into stony prejudice: on the one hand, fox-hunters are cruel, blood-thirsty sadists, viciously chasing a small, defenceless creature with a pack of 30 or 40 dogs; riding rough-shod over a cringing peasantry, they are as outdated in today's enlightened society as small swords and snuff: for the other half, antis are ignorant townees who know nothing of the countryside or its wildlife; mere rabble-rousers who are more engrossed with the destruction of a way of life than in exhibiting concern for foxes.

There is not the slightest doubt that much of the antagonism directed at foxhunting is based on class prejudice. The colourful dress of the hunting field, derived almost directly from the male costume of the early 19th century, invariably invokes a storm of abuse. Yet what *can* it possibly matter? One could, indeed, turn up at the meet dressed in dirty mac and wellington boots and mounted on a shaggy, ill-kempt cart-horse. Would this appease these radical, petty souls?

I care not a jot what anyone says. For my money there is still no more stirring or thrilling sight than a well-dressed and mounted field, perhaps gathered on a village green for the meet or moving across country. There is a poetry of movement and colour which in itself is sufficient answer to the mean-minded and critical. Red coats and black, silk hats and bowlers are a brittle contrast to the pastel greens and browns of the winter countryside; it is a cavalcade which can still stop, now more than ever before, the casual passer-by, aware perhaps that he is seeing something essentially English, something we cannot afford to lose.

Of course, there is glamour and tradition inextricably linked to the hunting field, but one most not overlook the central charge of cruelty which is constantly levelled at foxhunters.

Considered in isolation death in itself is cruel. The moment we deprive a creature — insect or elephant — of its life we have engaged in an act of cruelty. Those who pursue field sports must recognise this salient fact; they must also recognise, as should their opponents, that it is the aim of every field sportsman to reduce suffering to a minimum, to ensure a swift, clean death for whatever animal or bird he chooses as his quarry.

If we accept the above premise then we must also accept that there is cruelty in the farming of animals for domestic consumption. That the animal receives a swift end is irrelevant — the fact remains that we have organised its existence for our own purposes, denied it a decent life during its short span on earth and then killed it for food. Ah, say the antis, here is the crux of the thing — on the one hand we are forced to kill in order to maintain human life whilst on the other you kill merely for sport, for the enjoyment you derive from hunting a wild animal.

It is a hollow argument: death is final and to the creature killed it is totally irrelevant that the motives which result in its demise are derived from a desire for food or an ardour for the chase. A wild animal such as a fox is engaged in the business of killing from day to day, yet we must not ascribe to it a knowledge of death. This is the right only of humans — a foreknowledge which sets us above the animal kingdom. A hunted fox is seldom the pathetic picture conjured up by the antis; it is only in the last minute or so that fear may freeze and deaden its limbs; then the end is swift. The leading hound will roll it over, seizing the back and breaking the spine. The popular notion that the animal is torn to pieces while alive is a gross slur, one which any huntsman can refute.

The charge of sadism, of delighting in the death of an animal, is frequently hurled at those who follow hounds — it, too, is a baseless accusation. It is rare for the field to be up when a fox is rolled over in the open; far more likely they are still struggling across country two or three fields behind or winding their way through impenetrable woodland. A sadist following hounds with a view to indulging his perversion would soon retire unsatisfied.

So what then is it all about? Why this addiction which, for 200 or more years, has dominated the minds and bodies of hundreds of thousands of men and women, so that they have gladly devoted their entire lives to the sport, sacrificing perhaps health and wealth in the pursuit, but always content in the knowledge that they are maintaining a tradition which is an integral part of the British landscape, that they are prepared to accept the abundant risks, and that even though they bring death to a hunted animal — an animal which is itself a hunter — they do so swiftly and without causing the creature to suffer?

Being practical field sportsmen and conservationists foxhunters are well aware that foxes frequently have to be killed by snare or gun; there is simply no alternative. The dust-bin foxes, sleek and idle, that crowd the suburbs, must be kept down and there is only one answer; the keeper whose country is not hunted has no choice.

It is well worth emphasising that hunting a fox with hounds terminates in one of two ways — the animal is either cleanly killed outright or else it escapes unharmed, blown in the wind perhaps but with no other hurt.

I had not intended that this book, so delightfully illustrated by Alison Guest, should be an apology for hunting; no such apology is needed. The sport is controlled by an august body, the Masters of Foxhounds Association whose word is law throughout the foxhunting world in this country. The malpractices which in the past brought the good name of hunting into disrepute — bagged foxes and the practice of throwing a dug fox to hounds while alive — have long been proscribed and a good thing too.

No, this is not an apology, rather is it an attempt at an explanation, through words and pictures, of the background to foxhunting and all that goes to make this a 12-month way of life rather than a seasonal sport. The sportsman who, at the end of the season puts away his gun or turns out his hunter, content to take them up again at the end of the summer, having given scarcely a thought to his sport in the interim, misses an enormous amount of pleasure.

Like a diamond, foxhunting has many gleaming facets surrounding a central core of sheer excitement, that age-old joy in both seeing and hearing hounds, watching them puzzling the line, casting themselves and flinging on again in a frenzied peal of music which has no rival. This is the pleasure of the foot-follower, he who perhaps understands and loves hunting as much as any man and who, so often, if he knows his country, will see far more of the game than the mounted follower. Yet, for those of us who follow hounds on horseback, there is the additional appeal both of horsemanship, and that extra element of danger which adds a spice to the fun.

None of us wants to be hurt and we shudder with crossed fingers when we hear of broken limbs amongst friends or even — and it happens every season — of a fatal disaster. But, good heavens, if the element of risk were eliminated, if we were cocooned in a shell of certainty, would life be worth living?

Today the cost of hunting on horseback on a regular basis can be quite appalling. The days of a dozen hunters for the season with appropriate attendants have long melted away. Most people now keep one or two hunters which they do themselves with, perhaps, the assistance of a groom in the season.

In the days of our grandparents it was no doubt splendid to climb from one's second horse at the end of the day, to have it led away and to know that it would be cleaned, fed and rugged up, whilst we ourselves would be divested of our muddy garments which would vanish to some unknown region of the establishment for attention. Now, one is far more likely to be both groom and valet. Yet there is considerable pleasure to be derived from the knowledge that the gleaming, plaited horse, surmounted by your own clean, tidy self has been achieved with no outside assistance. It is hard work, and there comes a time, perhaps at the end of a tiresome day when everything has gone wrong, when you ask yourself if all the trouble and expense is really worth the effort? A few days later you answer the question as, once again, you go through the old familiar routine.

So, let's have a look behind the scenes to discover something of the intricate background to foxhunting, a background which, in its essentials has altered but little over the years.

Hunting today

A fact about foxhunting today, and a rather curious one, is that the sport should exist at all in this, the last quarter of the 20th century. After all, its imminent demise has been forecast for the past 150 years; the prophets of doom, the faint-hearted and weary, have, in turn, seized on the coming of the railways, the insidious encroachment of barbed-wire, the introduction of the internal combustion engine and the accelerating shrinkage of the countryside to convince themselves and their audience that the 'good old days' would never be repeated. Yet, somehow, foxhunting has survived these several crises. Not only survived but has proved beyond the shadow of doubt that, given goodwill, it can continue to exist on a perhaps modified but still virile basis.

There is no lack of support for foxhunting, not just from the rural community but also from many town dwellers who are sufficiently enlightened to appreciate that the sport embodies so much that is best in this country, so much that we hold dear. Is the secret of foxhunting the fact that in essence it is unchanging and has scarcely altered in two centuries? Those of us who ride to hounds can hardly ignore the fact that we are maintaining a tradition, that we are following precisely in the footsteps of our forefathers, doing as they did and feeling the same excitement that they knew.

The naïve, those who know nothing of the countryside or its traditional sports but who are guided solely in their opinion by the popular media, might suppose that the foxhunting community is a tiny, beleagured bastion of diehard, sadistic reactionaries clinging to their sport by a thread of influence and power. They might think so, just as they probably bracket grouse shooters as the wealthy, tweed-clothed red-faced colonel's brigade, but they would be totally and utterly wrong. Foxhunting today is bursting with life and enthusiasm. Support for the sport can occasionally prove almost embarassing and it is a regrettable fact that several hunts, particularly those in the south and south-east, are forced to close their subscription membership in order to keep the size of fields within reasonable bounds. The goodwill of the farming community is the keystone to foxhunting; lose this and then, truly, the sport has no future. Fortunately, despite attempts by the 'antis' to 'get at them', most farmers, by the nature of their calling, are a pretty level-headed lot, content to let the hunt on their land in the knowledge that any damage will be quickly repaired or, better still, they may take an active part in the sport.

Commonsense must be the guideline for a working relationship between the farming and hunting communities; in many areas fields of 150 to 200 are simply no longer acceptable and those who hunt on horseback should be aware that they are extremely fortunate. In my view, were it feasible to open the floodgates of hunting to all and sundry, active support for foxhunting would be far greater than is the case at the moment. In other words, foxhunting finds itself in the anomalous position of being so popular that, in order to preserve its good name it is forced, in many instances, to limit the mounted fields.

A few facts and figures are worth considering: today there are some 235 registered packs of foxhounds in the United Kingdom and Ireland and it may come as something of a surprise to a good many people to know that foxhunting is firmly entrenched in the U.S.A. where there are 130 packs, whilst Canada has 11 and there is even a pack of hounds in Mexico. Hunting is, of course, extremely popular in France where there are numerous packs pursuing deer, wild pig, hares and foxes with ceremony and tradition. One must not lose sight of the fact that there are also many packs of beagles, harriers and staghounds in this country, most of whom also find no lack of support, just the opposite.

One should not be blinded by numbers alone. Whilst, as I have mentioned, there is tremendous and growing support for foxhunting, despite assertions to the contrary from its opponents, the present economic climate is hardly calculated to encourage thoughts of expansion; rather is it a case of struggling to maintain standards by stringent economies. If we can mark time we will have done well.

Packs which hunted four days a week are thinking in terms of two or three, staff has had to be reduced and wastage cut back to the absolute minimum. All the petty, money-saving dodges which might have scarcely been considered a short while ago, are practised and Masters are forced to adopt the outlook of penny-pinching misers.

In a few cases packs have amalgamated; these ventures, despite the predictable moans from the pessimists, have generally proved successful. The reasons are usually associated with loss of land and it has invariably, and rightly, been considered that wherever possible foxhunting should be continued, even if it meant a reduction in kennels and staff. Far better to have an amalgamated hunt than no hunt at all.

There are few hunts today which do not, annually, scrutinise the cost of subscriptions and, usually, find themselves forced to increase them to keep pace with the cost of living. In my view, hunting is still relatively cheap in this country. Admittedly, if you do the thing on the grand scale, it can be enormously expensive but most of us, unable to rise to these heights, still stagger along, cutting costs wherever feasible; making that old coat and pair of boots do another season, though well aware that they should have been consigned to the bottom of the cupboard long since. The Dismal Jimmies constantly reiterate that sheer lack of finance will ultimately prove the ruination of hunting. They may well be right but I, personally, believe that wherever possible those who love hunting, horses, hounds and the countryside will be prepared to make sacrifices to ensure the continuation of the sport.

Few would be so foolish as to suggest that the future looks rosy, or has more than the faintest tinge of pink but, in the light of past events and the continual confounding of the pessimists, I firmly believe there is a future for foxhunting.

This faith has been reinforced over the past few years by concrete evidence of a rapport between shooting and hunting. For years it was generally accepted that there could be little love lost between the two field sports; each considered the other a damned nuisance and there was seldom more than token co-operation by either party, with the result that 'incidents' — hounds drawing coverts without due warning, foxes shot out of malice — were commonplace and, seized upon by the anti press at every opportunity.

The red light was glowing and, taking note of the danger signals, the British Field Sports Society, the Game Conservancy, and *Shooting Times and Country Magazine* promulgated a highly successful investigation into the actual effect of drawing coverts shortly before they were to be shot. The results were startling, convincing many who had hitherto been sceptical. Linked to exhibitions at Game Fairs and country shows, the campaign helped enormously to bring both sides together and, most important of all, convince them that they were both on the same side of the fence. Today a fresh and healthy atmosphere prevails between hunting and shooting; of course there are still exceptions on both sides; those who will not, and cannot, see beyond their own parishes or pockets.

Opponents of foxhunting almost invariably aim their shafts at the 'shire' hunts — the Quorn, the Pytchley, the Cottesmore, the Belvoir — confident that the smartly turned-out fields can be used to foster the tired old *cliché* of class prejudice. Yet it is a fact, and there is no gainsaying this, that foxhunting, and hunting in general, is the most democratic of sports. Not all those who follow hounds ride, or even want to ride. Take a survey of a field, mounted, on foot and car-borne, and you will come up with a cross-section of the population; all trades, types, so-called classes and stratas of society will be represented, each as good as the other and all bound together by a common link — a love for the best of all sports.

There are small hunts, there are large hunts, there are farmers' hunts, there are smart hunts, there are 'working' hunts and suburban hunts; there are foot-packs and half-and-half packs, and there is scarcely a corner of these Isles, apart from the rugged north and extreme west and parts of the eastern counties, which does not have its resident pack, each with its stalwart supporters, each sure that it can provide sport of a special character and most with a history, often going back one or two hundred years.

The eight Fell packs, all of which are hunted on foot, present a singularly nasty problem for the antis and one which they choose to avoid whenever possible. Here, in the rugged fells, foxes are a definite menace to the sheep farmers, and despite assertions to the contrary there is overwhelming evidence to show that they destroy a considerable number of lambs each season. Foxes cannot be shot, snared, poisoned or gassed by reason of the terrain — the only answer, and a highly successful one, is to employ hounds. Indeed, the hunts are normally on call into the early part of the summer should a farmer find himself in trouble.

I have said that foxhunting is democratic and so it is. Anyone is more than welcome to join his local hunt, supporting it through either the supporters' club or through some other category, though he must not automatically expect to be able to follow hounds on horseback for, as previously explained, this may not always be immediately possible.

Supporting your local hounds means more, far more, than merely paying a subscription and turning out at half-a-dozen meets during the season. Whatever your category of support, you will, if keen, find that you are involved in an annual round of sporting and social events; if a stranger to the countryside nothing is more likely to provide you with a sense of 'belonging' than support for the hunt. If you are inclined you will soon find yourself being roped in for numerous duties, for the hunt which operates like a well-oiled machine is the one which relies on active and capable supporters.

The Hunt Supporters' Club today plays an essential role in most hunts, enabling the supporter who prefers to follow hounds on foot or by car or bike to play an active, and often vital part, in the welfare and maintenance of the hunt. Active clubs organize a wide variety of fund-raising events throughout the year, ranging from raffles, dinners, auctions, to material assistance in running the point-to-point and open day at the Kennels. The latter is always great fun, a time for relaxation and the supporters usually play a major part in manning the numerous produce stalls and, particularly, the terrier show and racing.

Terrier shows are still enormous fun provided they are not taken too seriously. Unfortunately, in recent years, there has been a tendency for 'pot-hunters' to 'do' the shows, frequently displaying a marked lack of sportsmanship if all does not go their way. Working terriers are invariably a source of controversy, but it is pleasing to note that there is a strong move back to the 'real' working terrier stamp, the 'Heinz' variety proving less popular with terrier folk who know the score.

The sums raised for the hunt by the Supporters' Club are often quite astonishing, enabling them to purchase new trailers for horse or hounds or perhaps a Land-Rover. Without supporters few hunts could today look with any degree of assurance to the future.

Personally I believe that foxhunting — and hunting in general — would obtain and hold far wider support amongst the general public if only it could improve both its image and lines of communication. Until fairly recently press reports of 'incidents' have usually been exaggerated out of all proportion, the emotive and colourful language and descriptions of the all too vociferous spokesman from the antis, capturing the headlines.

Foxes are invariably 'torn to pieces by the dogs', the implication, of course, being that they are alive at the time; huntsmen lash at hounds and the public with their whips and the field ride 'rough-shod' and with total indifference to the feelings of other road users. 'Sadistic', 'cruel', 'dressing up to kill'; how tired we become of hearing these worn old *clichés* trotted out with the regularity of seaside donkeys.

Fortunately, a breath of fresh air has blown through the hunting world, bringing with it a new awareness that, if hunting is to survive, it must be prepared to explain and re-educate a public which has been fed on distorted propaganda for years. It is no easy task but, given the resources, there is no doubt that truth will prevail. The British public are by no means as foolish or gullible as the antis would like to believe.

I have always found that if, when attacked on a question of field sports, one takes time and trouble to explain the facts, dispelling the myths as one goes along, one can usually dislodge a good many of the prejudices and half-baked notions. Occasionally one even gains a convert.

Summer idyll

For the hunt servant his hour of glory comes with the opening meet
in November; then, resplendent in bright scarlet and polished boots
with spurs winking, jauntily bestriding a well turned out hunt horse,
the world is indeed sweet. Less glamorous are the long hours spent in
kennel, cleaning yards, attending to whelping bitches, walking out
hounds, exercising, collecting flesh and skinning swollen corpses. It is
a year-long ritual which provides, if anything, almost more work for
the hunt staff in the summer than during the hunting season.

The spring and summer months are a time of shows — puppy, hound and terrier; a time to raise funds for the hunt, to parade hounds at innumerable country fairs and occasions; it is the time of the point-to-point and the hunter trials, gymkhanas, jumble sales and auctions.

It is indeed a period of considerable activity, a breathing space for consolidation, rest and recovery, but for hounds the long, hot days are spent dreaming and dozing on their benches.

For most hunts the season comes to an end in March, though a few, able to take hounds to the hills and away from the spring sowing or where the moors present few hazards, may continue right through to the end of April. Most horses, though, will probably have suffered sufficient wear and tear by the early spring, especially if it has been a dry, hard winter; a crop of filled legs and sprains will soon have the stud groom counting the days to the final meet.

Co-operation between the hunt and the local shoots is of the utmost importance; the smooth running of both sports will only occur if each is prepared to bend and give a little in the other's favour. The keepers are a loyal, trustworthy fraternity and only occasionally, like a rotten apple in a barrel, will a sour one turn up, but when he does immense harm can be caused.

The spring is a time to say 'thank you' to the local keepers. They have their jobs and naturally their first loyalties must be to the men who employ and pay them, but an understanding employer, even if he is not a hunting man, will realise that both sports have a place in the countryside and he will wish to know that his keeper can ensure a fox in covert when hounds draw the main coverts. Intelligent keepers are well aware that, although not ideal neighbours, pheasants can still be shown with little significant loss despite a litter or two of cubs on the estate. One friend of mine, a man of decided views and opinions, rears his 1500 birds each season and will not permit a fox to be killed, yet in no way has his shooting declined and the hunt is always sure of a find.

So the keepers' lunch and clay pigeon shoot is now a regular feature with most hunts — and what if the keepers invariably beat the hunt teams? It is the spirit of the thing that counts. A small enough affair of rural life, little known and less cared about by the bustling mass. Yet these minor moments, these social occasions, ensure that the structure of the hunt and its intricate relationships with the rural community are sound and good for another year.

In May hounds will be graded for the puppy shows in June and July. There is a certain something about the puppy show which embodies the essence of the England most of us still recall and can recapture in these brief glimpses of a golden age. It is very much a club gathering, the proud puppy walkers eyeing their erstwhile charges, now so mature and very much animals of the kennel; the hunt servants from neighbouring counties, sombre in the regulation uniform of dark suit and bowler, while Masters and the elders of the hunt adopt the slightly rakish Panama hat. Hounds display themselves on the flags, are criticised and considered, breed lists are consulted and much wisdom and, perhaps a little nonsense, is bandied round the ring. And then perhaps a tea-party on the lawn, a look at kennels and next week one will be visiting an adjacent county to see what *they* have to offer.

Someone once remarked that the puppy-walkers are the backbone of a hunt — well perhaps so, and let's throw in the farmers for good measure. But certainly, few hunts could really operate an efficient and economic breeding policy were it not for these stalwart folk.

Each spring they collect their couple of whelps, fat bundles with a number tattooed in one ear and already bent on mischief; though, I must confess that, in our fourth season of puppy-walking, the minor moments of stress, the odd holes in the lawn, the shredded washing, the shrieking hens, are worth every minute of the joy brought to the farm for three-quarters of the year. It is always a sad moment when they return to kennel and the talk for the next few months is all of the couple to come.

For most hunts today the point-to-point is an important source of revenue and a wash-out, with poor attendance as a result, can prove a shattering blow to the nerves of the hunt treasurer. The season begins in early February and runs right through to June.

It is perhaps rather more than just a pity that the point-to-point has lost much of its former character. Originally intended as a race for members' own hunt horses and ridden in hunting clothing, it has now become little more than a minor hunter chase; fences are carefully made up on an artificial course and the riders and their mounts are so designed, in many cases, for the racing rather than the hunting world. It is a world of bookmakers and the tote, of hunting folk and jolly holiday crowds out for a breath of country air, a mild flutter and the excitement of the spills and tumbles which mark most meetings. I suppose one should be rather more enthusiastic but I feel that already the whole affair has become totally divorced in the eye of the public from the hunting image. This is indeed a great pity for it is one day in the year when the crowds can support the hunt and be seen to be doing it.

A new event, cross-country riding is, in my view, recapturing much of the excitement lost by the point-to-point. Basically, teams of four take a line across a set course of natural fences, the fastest time based on the third member of a team home, being the winner. Courses are usually about $2\frac{1}{2}$ miles with 20 or so fences; these vary according to the importance of the competition but in many cases small alternative jumps are provided to enable the less expert rider or novice to get round.

So far cross-country events have not been subjected to a plethora of rules and regulations and there is, praise be, no governing body. Part of the pleasure is the fact that formality is kept to a minimum and that, if one wishes, one can ride the course in hunting clothes rather than crash-helmets and colours.

And so the summer marches on and with it come those splendid occasions, the hound shows, starting with, to my southern mind, one one of the most delightful of all, Ardingly. Here, at the South of England Show held in early June the foxhounds are shown on the Thursday and the beagles on the Friday. The small ring, the covered stand and the cluster of tents and caravans close by the entrance to the Showground draw Masters, hunt servants and dedicated hunting folk from all over the country; it is a likeable, friendly show, lacking the majesty of Peterborough or the scenery of Rydal but in its own quiet, southern, Sussex way it is a charming start to the show season.

These hound shows, what fun they are! Each has a charm of its own and each, like a London club, has its regulars and old-stagers, men and women who have been coming for years, assured that the familiar faces will, once again, revive memories, sadly aware that one or two, each summer, are no longer there to take their places by the ringside, but ever conscious of the continuity and the sense that here is something that, like the most enduring and best of institutions, changes only in the actors, never the play.

One of the most magnetic moments, one which seldom fails to catch my eye at a hound show is the sight of a hunt servant, polished and smart, standing on the flags, linked by an invisible thread to his adoring hound; a slight movement of the hands and those brown eyes feast him as, head cocked slightly, his charge stands there, well aware that he or she is the sole centre of attraction. That link between man and hound is the secret of which a huntsman can make so much or so little. It is the same understanding, a speech of minds, which joins the gundog trainer and his animal, the horsemaster and his mount.

By the middle of July hound exercising is once again under way. The hunt staff use bicycles in order to avoid getting the horses up from grass too early. At first 45 minutes steady roadwork is enough but soon it is worked up to two hours and by the second week in August the horses, pig-fat from four months of loafing in the meadows, are being walked out with hounds. For them the long summer sleep is over; the hours of dozing in the shade of the oaks, head to rump, tails monotonously flicking flies from each other's heads, all these will again become a memory. The old round is gently easing its way into active life.

For the Master, who may, of course, be huntsman, too, the summer is a time for doing the 'rounds'. Farmers and keepers must be visited, problems discussed, relationships strengthened and plans formulated for the coming season. It is a period of planning and adjustment. There may be opportunities for opening up new country, provided the right approach is taken. A good, active Master, with an open, genuine air can do wonders for a country. Most folk, even the most awkward, or ones with reputations for being real bad 'uns, will, if tackled in the right way, quite often come up trumps. All too regularly problems have been caused through thoughtlessness and a total inability to see the other man's point of view.

A Master who takes swift action will seldom have a great deal of trouble on his hands. I know one man who makes a point of seeing a farmer or landowner, a village woman or keeper, the night of an alleged incident. Wheat ridden over, hounds in a forbidden covert, a terrified cat, or hounds through a back garden; they may seem of minor moment to the field but to the people concerned they mean a great deal and, unless the Master pours soothing oil, these troubled waters can quickly swell to a raging surf to be seized on by the journalist. Before one knows what has happened a trivial affair is making headlines in the press.

Come August there is a feeling of expectation in kennels. Cubhunting is just round the corner, horses are slowly being brought up and the hounds are beginning to sharpen. The talk is all of the harvest, though for a handful of packs who hunt in forest or moor these hot, late summer days will already have seen a start made in the education of hounds and foxes. For most a late harvest means a correspondingly late start to cubhunting and then it is, perhaps, almost impossible to cover all the country before the season proper gets under way. The result may be complaints from poulty keepers and farmers suffering poultry losses; whilst drawing a covert which has not been cubhunted may result in frustration as foxes gallop in all directions to the delight of the more excitable members of the field, as the chorus of holloas from all quarters testifies.

By the calendar it is still summer and the holiday crowds are splashing and loafing in the sun, but for some of us thoughts are already being cast forward to the cool, crisp dawns of autumn when the mists come up from meadows and the hedgerows are heavy with berries. Cubhunting and the old, familiar round are with us once again. . . .

Cubhunting again

The happiest man in England, wrote Will Ogilvie, rose an hour before the dawn. I always recall those simple lines on the first cubhunting morning of a new season; hunting proper, in all its full-blown fig, is still some two months away, but at least one is again astride a horse: one will again see and hear hounds and the old magic, that age-old spell, is once again weaving its singular charm.

I always catch a hint of something of our primitive, distant past in rising long before the sun is timed to lighten the eastern sky. There is a peace, a stillness, a sense of attachment to all those thousands of dawns seen by our forefathers when the horse was still the dominant means of locomotion.

There is also something immensely comforting in the orange glow from the loose boxes and a pleasure to be taken in the heads peering over half-doors, each horse wondering at the unwanted disturbance. But only the big grey, that old-fashioned Irishman, knows that once again it is time to prove his real reason for living. No idle hack he, no leaper in rings or round courses; he only comes alive at the sound of the horn and the sight of hounds. Like a true Irishman he is an inveterate sportsman, but it must, for him, be the real thing.

Tack, lovingly oiled and polished, supple and deep brown, is aboard, the trailer is hitched, and with a clatter of hooves across the black and orange yard, raising a creaky murmur of admonition from the roosting guinea-fowl, the grey is led to the ramp. The brake is checked and, with a final glance to make sure bowler and whip are present, the Land-Rover throbs through the gate and onto the road.

It is half-light when we unbox; a greyish dawn with a few coiled wisps of mist hanging over the meadows and a clear sky to promise a golden day, as glorious as only early September days can be. The harvest is all gathered in now and already some of the stubbles have been turned in, brown against pale gold as the sun's red disc creeps above the distant hills. It is still chilly and the rhythmical trotting of the grey as we hack to the meet, powerful shoulders swinging smoothly, brings a glow to hands and face.

The meet is a mere triangle of green by a cross-roads but it has brought a dozen or so of the really keen ones from their beds. Familiar faces, quiet greetings and a general feeling of deep pleasure that once again we are in action.

The major's wife is there as usual, mounted on the big bay with a kick in him like a mule if you don't watch out; the little horse dealer, Tommy, nigh 70, is astride a nervous, rakish-looking four-year-old which, he tells you confidentially, has never seen hounds before but should be alright. There's a nervous twitch about its quarters, though, which makes you thank your stars it's between his more than competent legs and not yours. Two or three young faces on ponies still pot-bellied from the summer grass; the dapper gent who never misses a meet, on foot or on horse and who always emerges at the end of a day with scarce a fleck of mud on his neat person, and the hard-riding lady on the chestnut that won't jump — they're all there and all ready to agree it's a blessing the summer is over and time to get on with business.

And who's that small, tweedy, fellow talking knowingly and confidentially to another equally small and rather varminty man? The two broken-coated terriers straining on taut leashes betray their calling, though let's hope we've no work for them today.

A stir amongst the tiny field, a distant rate and the clatter of hooves, as hounds are brought on; it is the bitches this morning, $16\frac{1}{2}$ couple of as pretty blacks, tans and whites as you'll find anywhere — or at least so Tom our huntsman will gladly tell you. They're an evenly marked pack on the whole, with just two light hounds and one of the blue-mottled strain. The hours of summer walking and discipline have proved their value for even when we trot on to the first covert hounds keep well together, though we pause as one after another they empty themselves on the verge.

Cubhunting has its critics — and one can, to some extent, sympathise with their superficial assessments. It is unfortunate, I think, that to the uninformed, the very name itself suggests the chivvying of very young, near helpless foxes, fluffy cubs still dependent on their mother. The truth is, of course, that come September, which usually sees the start of cubhunting, though much depends on the harvest for little can be done till the corn is in, the young foxes are well-grown and more than capable of taking care of themselves.

The exercise has several objects, not the least of which is to break up the litters and try to thin them out. Unless this is done there would be far too many foxes in one covert, creating confusion when hunting proper and possibly also bringing complaints from farmers and keepers.

The young hounds, those which entered the pack from walk the previous spring, must also be taught their job — namely to hunt fox and nothing but fox. Older, experienced hounds must be taken out with the youngsters to teach them by example. For a young hound his first entry into a covert will be a confusing and exciting moment. A *pot pourri* of enticing smells will assail him; a pheasant clattering up with an outraged 'cock-up' will startle, a flashing grey form may bend his mind to rabbit. Worst of all, deer may be present, those cloven-hooved nightmares, dreaded by all huntsmen.

The scent of roe or fallow is particularly alluring, occasionally causing even the most staunch of hounds to give way. It is curious how the note of hounds changes when on the line of deer; they throw tongue with a wilder, more hysterical note, easily recognised with experience. Deer are indeed the very devil and their rapid increase in many counties, especially in the south, has caused a great many problems. My own hunt is sufficiently fortunate to have their kennels in parkland in which roams a large herd of fallow deer. The young hounds walked out in the summer, quickly become familiar with the deer, treating them with indifference. In one or two other countries, however, where deer have scarcely been known till recent years, a good many foxes have saved their brushes by the unwitting alliance of fallow or roe.

Cubhunting is much the Master's prerogative and, by tradition, although they are normally most welcome, the field are there by invitation and not of right. Although in October foxes may be allowed to break covert and the pack laid on in the normal fashion, in September it is very much a case of holding up. The field, such as it is, of perhaps only a dozen or so riders and as many on foot, will surround the covert, keeping at least 50 yards from its boundary. Any closer and a fox will slip through the ring without hindrance.

Old foxes will almost invariably break covert at once and no amount of tapping on saddles or 'hi hi Charlies' will turn them — and rightly, too. The young foxes with courage and determination will also escape, leaving the weaker and less mentally agile to fall. Once well stirred up, the youngsters that have departed will, in the future, leave covert at top speed to find refuge elsewhere.

It is, indeed, an education for the young entry for they will have not only to learn to resist all smells but the intoxicating whiff of fox, but will also discover how to negotiate the country, crawling, wriggling through brambles, creeping under gates and jumping netting. And all the time the huntsman and his whips will be marking with keen interest the promising, the hopefuls and the doubtfuls. This is perhaps the first time that the young hounds will have left the huntsman's heels and there may well be one or two shy hounds which still hang round his horse. They will probably soon catch on, though, diving into covert as eagerly as the rest.

Cubhunting is the formative period for young hounds, the time when they will learn to hunt, use their noses, to obey the huntsman by voice or horn. Those that fail to meet his standards, the babblers, the mute runners, the skirters, will be drafted to drag hunts where these vices are of little account, whilst the uneven and the misfits will be put down or drafted to other hunts who may not be too particular.

It is a time of learning for the young; for hounds, for foxes and for horses, too, for there is no better means of introduction to the hunting field for a green horse. It will have to learn discipline, to stand patiently for many minutes at a time, to understand that hounds are its allies and other horses its companions in the chase. Fretting is natural enough in a youngster, full of himself and wondering at the strange sights and sounds, but it is far better he acquires his experience when fields are small and the disciplines of hunting proper are not quite so rigidly enforced. People who bring out a young horse in November are little short of a menace for it is then too late to instil a placid temperament, and someone, or someone else's horse, will suffer.

The ideals of cubhunting cannot always be put into practise, usually because a country simply does not lend itself to holding up coverts. On Exmoor, for instance, the coverts are few and far between but hunts, on the other hand, can get under way earlier for there is no corn to suffer and somehow they teach their stout moor foxes the tricks of the game in less than no time.

In some of the southern countries, too, the woodlands are too big and too many for successful holding up, so a compromise situation results, small coverts being held up and the bigger woods being hunted properly.

On the other hand, in the Shires, coverts may be held up in orthodox fashion till late October.

It is quiet in covert. Only the huntsman's encouraging voice, and an occasional touch on the horn and the rasp of a jay and hysterical *chirk, chirk* of a blackbird break the hush. A puppy runs out of the wood, followed by another, brown eyes gaze blankly at horses and riders, then as one they dart back.

Abruptly there is a whimper, quickly followed by a rate and pistol-like crack of a whip as a youngster chases a rabbit or hare. But there is a litter here, for they have been watched in the summer evenings and dawns, and now old Priestess confirms their presence. 'Hike, hike, hike to Priestess', an encouraging rattle on the horn and then like the crashing of a mighty wave on the shore, a chorus of music swells, increasing and diminishing in volume as a leash of cubs are chivvied round the wood.

'Tally ho bike' as a cub ventures into the open, then pops back; another slips down a drain and into a hedgerow. A good fox this and like enough he'll lead us a merry dance when winter comes. A crashing crescendo of hound music fades abruptly as a cub is caught and the huntsman's distant whoop confirms the opening tally.

Cubhunting has an additional delight, the sheer pleasure of being abroad in the dawn before the world has stirred itself; it is a time when nature is unguarded and the sight of a roe doe and fawn bounding from a covert, rabbits lining the hedgerows and pheasants strutting in all their mailed glory is compensation enough for the early rise.

Hounds please . . .

'Opening Meet' — the simple words are the climax to the hunting year. All the weeks of walking puppies, the various shows, the summer exercise, the getting fit, the autumn cubhunting days; all the hard work for Master and secretary, the rounds of farmers, the diplomacy and tact, all culminate in that day at the beginning of November, when for those who follow hounds, whatever their means of locomotion, life once again takes on an extra meaning.

The autumn is now rolling on apace; the mornings are dull and moist, with brief hints of fog, early morning frosts clamp frozen fingers on the garden and the leaves, red and brown, crisp and curled, are stripped from branch and twig by fitful gusts. Only the oak clings grimly to the tattered remnants of its summer glory. There are haws in the hedges and the holly is already speckled with scarlet-like drops of sealing wax.

The Opening Meet! What a frenzy of polishing, clipping, plaiting, cleaning, repairing and replacing. Jobs which we fully intended to complete before the summer was out have somehow crept upon us unawares and the saddler is kept busy, stitching and cutting for hours on end. The brown boots of cubhunting have been put aside, replaced by the treasured top-boots, their gleaming sides and toes scored by a hundred thorn hedges. Patched and worn, they still carry a fine polish, reflecting hours of elbow-grease with bone or silk pad. Never let a brush touch your boots; it will break up the thin film of polish imparted by persistent hard work.

Saddle and tack are supple and well oiled, the horse is coming fit and looks a picture in his hunter clip, a network of veins on rippling muscle. He, too, knows that today is rather special; when we mount to hack on to the meet from the trailer, he steps out with a jaunty stride, conscious that once again there is a red coat on his back.

Perhaps, like me, you are your own groom, chauffer and valet; a neat turn-out, sufficient to catch the eye, may well be the result of literally hours of work during the week. Sometimes at the end of a day, when one surveys the damage, most of it in the shape of mud, plastering the horse and self, one is tempted to throw in the sponge. Ours is a singularly wet, clay-bottomed country so that the result of a week's rain has to be seen to be believed, One ill-placed hoof in a puddle of mud, from your horse or passing rider, will instantly destroy a pristine appearance. But it is all of no consequence. How can it be weighed against the thrill of the sport?

The Opening Meet may be held at an inn, at the Kennels, or as a lawn meet. Wherever it is you may be sure of a maximum turn-out. There will be faces one may not see again all season and, of course, there will be all the old familiar ones, a few not seen since the end of last season, though most will have put in an appearance at the shows in the summer, or enjoyed a few days cubhunting.

Is it any wonder that a meet of hounds in a truly English setting still attracts scores of onlookers? There is all the drama and colour of a well-rehearsed play whose outcome is ever in the balance. Red coats and black, silk hats, bowlers and caps; breedy quads stamp and snort nervously while their more phlegmatic cold-blooded cousins take it all in their stride; children, some in jodphurs, others in boots, straddle ponies which run the whole gamut of the pony world. There are Thelwell ponies, hairy and wild-maned, cobby little fellows and one or two miniature thoroughbred types; some from the moors, some from the best stables, other from Heaven knows where! But all relishing every second.

What a cluster of folk round the hounds! Trays of ports and sherry are lofted by a dozen foot-followers, cameras click and cines whirr as, for the umty-umpth time, the Master, huntsman and whips are recorded for the benefit of the local press and scores of albums.

With a field this size — 150 horses perhaps — it is well worth ensuring that caps and field money have been collected. Only the puppy-walkers escape, for it is agreed that their stalwart efforts should be rewarded with amnesty where field money is concerned.

Now there is a stir among the crowd and horses. With a touch on the horn our huntsman leads hounds through the throng, glad enough, no doubt, to be clear of the horses and to know his precious charges have avoided heels.

Kicking is the curse of the hunting field. It is a pound to a pinch of snuff that someone or a horse will be at the receiving end of a horse-shoe in the course of a day's hunting. The potential trouble-makers should carry a red warning in their tails, but this is seldom good enough, for their riders, on whom the responsibility lies, instead of making every effort to keep their ill-mannered nags at the rear of the field and well away from other horses, are too often inclined to assume that a ribbon is warning enough, and the onus lies on other riders to steer clear.

Most accidents occur in gateways when horses are crowding through or in rides of a wood when, perhaps, the field is waiting for hounds to draw on. Only those who have been kicked on the shin or ankle know the excruciating agony, and broken limbs as a result are not infrequent. Leather will to some extent absorb the blow, but rubber is useless and one reason amongst several why I dislike rubber boots.

Damage to one's horse is even more infuriating and no apology can repay a swollen knee or badly cut leg, resulting in a laid-up horse and expensive vet's bills.

Opening Meets do not usually conform to the rules of good hunting. There are too many riders, car and foot-followers for comfort, foxes are likely to be headed and to run in rings and the swollen field is a Field Master's nightmare. But we must suppose that on this our Opening Day we are blessed with Fortune, an accommodating field and a fox willing to travel.

The first covert drawn is blank, much to the astonishment of the local keeper who has already wagered a pint on Charlie being at home. A warm three acres of Scots firs with a comfortable patch of rhododendrons in the middle, it is rare, indeed, for a fox to be found 'away'. Yet one can never be absolutely certain and today is the exception.

On then, trotting down a side road for nearly half-a-mile to an eight-acre field of kale. Sited close to the farm buildings, it is surrounded on all sides by closely-clipped thorn hedges stretching away in a chequered pattern to a distant vale and the winding glint of a willow-lined brook. There are post-and rail hunt jumps in corners of most fields, but the hedges are eminently jumpable; clean, with no wire and a ditch on the far side, they are a pleasure to behold. Already a flask or two is out and eyes are being cast at the most favourable line.

The huntsman keeps to the edge of the kale, quietly encouraging hounds to draw up-wind. Only the waving plants and the odd glimpse of a head or stern marks their progress. The field are huddled in a corner, the inveterate 'coffee-housers' giving their tongues brisk exercise, while the thrusters and hardened old-stagers are keeping a sharp eye on the edge of the kale. On the far side the two whips can be seen, still as statues. Foot-followers crowd the road, a line of parked cars stretching away up the lane.

Silence. For ten minutes or more nerves are strained and then, when the whisper of 'blank again' is beginning to circulate, there comes a faint whimper, a firmer confirmation and suddenly the whole pack are giving tongue. But this fox is no stranger to hunting and is well aware of the mischief that awaits a tardy withdrawal. Running just on the inside of the kale, twice he over-runs the line, nips into a ditch, is headed back by a foot-follower then breaks at the top end.

Oh! The thrill of that screeching holloa from the first whipper-in; aloft in the saddle, cap raised, he has seen the lithe brown form streak across the field and through the far hedge. Before hounds can be laid on Charlie is a field and a half to the good. Comes a staccato doubling of the horn, the hounds surge forward and the 'for-forraard awaaay' tells us all we want to know. There is an excited surging in the field, the bold edging forward, the more cautious finding a sudden need to examine girths or leathers, while the foot-followers trot back to their cars.

The huntsman has popped over the first hedge, one whipper-in has galloped away to the right and the second is bringing on two couple of laggard hounds. The Field Master drops his white-gloved hand and away we go!

In countries where jumping is mostly confined to hunt jumps with the attendant queues of sweaty, fidgety horses, when the occasional hedge does present itself, there is an unfortunate tendency for the field to play follow-my-leader, usually resulting in a hole being punched through the hedge and repair work for the fence-builders. It is far better to spread out in a hedged country, each rider picking his own spot and sticking to it. Swerving horses are a damnable nuisance and likely to cause accidents.

Already the first hedge has taken its toll, two loose horses are cantering across the field, their riders dusting off the dirt. The tail of cars has almost disappeared, the terrier man's Land-Rover in the lead and suddenly, almost abruptly, the landscape is empty. Few things vanish so swiftly as a hunt, as those who have lost hounds and searched for an hour or more, will readily testify.

Jumping the hedges as they come, the field quickly telescopes, the slower and more cautious taking advatage of made-up jumps or gates; the pace, for four fields, is astonishing, the cry of hounds growing ever fainter then, to the general relief, there is a check. A field of plough has brought hounds to their noses. Quietly the huntsman encourages them to cast themselves, chirruping softly to them, as they fan out. A whimper from old Rallywood and the remainder swing as one, pick up the line and press on down the headlands towards a small spinney. A deep, wide ditch on the take-off side and a really broad hedge deters all but the most hardy. A young girl tries it first, but her horse doesn't spread out, landing across the hedge and tossing her over. Fortunately a gate is to hand and riders jostle with impatience as they see hounds running again from the far side of the spinney.

Away again with a variety of hazards to negotiate before our fast burst away from the kale ends, perhaps, with our pilot marked to ground in a drain or unstopped earth, though if hounds can really get on terms with him and there is a serving scent, he may be rolled over in the open — a quick snap from the leading hound, a worry and it is all finished. If Charlie has, indeed, gone to ground and *if* the Master decides that he should be bolted or dispatched, according to the requirements of the country, the terrier man will appear on the scene like magic. In many countries the terrier man and his tough little assistants may play a vital part if foxes are to be killed. In a heavily wooded country, where it is perhaps virtually impossible to 'stop' the earths, foxes are likely to get to ground more often than most, few being killed by hounds above ground. The majority will probably be killed with a humane killer.

If it is decided that a fox should be bolted, then hounds must be kept back and the quarry given reasonable Law.

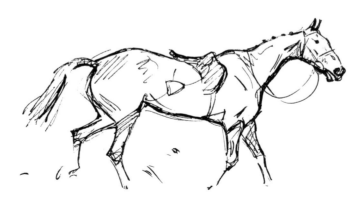

What a gathering of steaming horses and red-faced riders cast up in dribs and drabs, the front runners recounting their adventures to anyone who will listen as the huntsman doubles his horn. Odd snatches of conversation tell of missing glasses, a broken collar-bone, a horse wedged in a ditch . But all is soon righted — the glasses again adorn their owner, the collar-bone is only a sprain and the stricken horse has righted itself unaided.

Few sights in the hunting field are more pathetic than a winded horse, collapsed on its side or inverted in a ditch. Its last moment appears to be imminent and it will make not the slightest effort to struggle up, but seems resigned to its fate. Given a chance to catch its breath, though, it will make a violent effort to struggle to its feet, probably none the worse.

And so hounds will move on to draw the next covert and already, even though it is but an hour or so since the meet, one or two riders are slipping away, perhaps content in the knowledge that they have had a run and survived the course. It is always a source of wonderment to me that by two o'clock most hunting fields are reduced by half their number; there are, of course, those who come out only to be seen or to exercise a horse, there are also folk who tell you that they enjoy every minute of the fun, who go to endless time and expense to ensure that they appear at the meet on time as smart as a new button yet who seldom, if ever, stay the course. So often the best of the day comes in the late afternoon when the sun is sinking and a cold waft of air seems to bring with it a fresh vigour to scent. Besides these folk miss the quiet pleasure of hacking back to the trailer or box in the gathering dusk; one feels relaxed and content, watching hounds trot in front, the huntsman or whip making sure they keep well to the side of the road with up-raised whip.

For the man who is his own groom there is still much to be done before he can retire to the bath with a large gin and tonic. The horse must be attended to first; food, a light grooming and careful check for any thorns, cuts or other damage, a warm bed, plenty of water and rugs and bandages will keep him fair for the morning, with a late night check to make sure he has not broken out and is resting quietly.

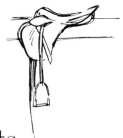

Miscellany of meets

It is, I suppose, perfectly natural over the years the spotlight of public attention has been focussed on the Shires, that Mecca of foxhunting which even in the early years of the 19th century when Nimrod (Charles Apperley) was conducting his hunting tours, had acquired a resounding fame.

High Leicestershire, with its strongly enclosed pastures, its lack of plough and woodland, its small coverts and its reasonably accessible situation contained (and to a considerable extent still retains) all that an ardent rider to hounds could desire.

The provinces, those countries outside the Shires, were looked upon and spoken of with a shade of condescension — they were tremendous fun, each possesssed its own peculiar charm and merit, but for the real thing, well, one simply had to head for the Midlands.

The Shires still, today, hold pride of place but there are many countries which can show sport of an equally high order even though they lack the physical advantages. One thinks of the plough countries of the east, those extensive fields bisected by ditches and where long points are frequently the order of the day; there are the wide and fearsome rhines of the Somerset levels; the stout black hedges of the Dorset vales; the on-and-off banks of the far West; the moorlands and grassland of the north-east; the dense woodlands of the southern counties with their deep, glutinous rides and overhanging branches, and the stone-wall counties where a horse must be able to gallop on. In the Lake District and Fells, the foot-packs whose success is so vital to the sheep-farmers at lambing time, have hazards of mountain loose scree and sudden mists with which to contend.

But wherever and whatever the country, there will exist a genuine community spirit, a sense of belonging and a burning desire to ensure that hunting continues, a 300-year-old sport which embodies all that is best in this country. For its adherents foxhunting is truly a way of life, and I can only hope that this book has conveyed something of the real spirit, the meaning, of an activity which has, in recent years, suffered the attentions of the ignorant, the foolish, and the embittered.